# THREE-IN-ONE

## THE UNITY OF THE FATHER, SON, AND HOLY SPIRIT

ISBN 978-1-0877-5218-1
Item 005834395
Dewey Decimal Classification Number: 242
Subject Heading: DEVOTIONAL LITERATURE / BIBLE STUDY AND TEACHING / GOD

Printed in the United States of America

Student Ministry Publishing
Lifeway Resources
One Lifeway Plaza
Nashville, Tennessee 37234

We believe that the Bible has God for its author; salvation for its end; and truth, without any mixture of error, for its matter and that all Scripture is totally true and trustworthy. To review Lifeway's doctrinal guideline, please visit www.lifeway.com/doctrinalguideline.

# publishing team

*Director, Student Ministry*
Ben Trueblood

*Manager, Student Ministry Publishing*
John Paul Basham

*Editorial Team Leader*
Karen Daniel

*Writer*
Jesse Campbell

*Content Editor*
Kyle Wiltshire

*Production Editor*
Brooke Hill

*Graphic Designer*
Shiloh Stufflebeam

# TABLE OF CONTENTS

# INTRO

The experts say your generation loves a challenge. Since you are not afraid of challenges, step into the most challenging doctrine in all of Christianity—the doctrine of the Trinity. It is a beautiful mystery. There is no illustration that perfectly explains the reality that God exists as three equal, divine Persons, united in one mysterious bond of love. If we try to reduce the Trinitarian nature of God into terms we can neatly understand, all our attempts fall short of His glorious reality. If we fill in the blanks of our understanding with ideas of our own making, we do not honor the truth of our God. So why should we tackle such an intense doctrine? Because the truth is out there. And it's found in the Bible.

Theologians have marveled at the unity and simultaneous distinctiveness of the Father, Son, and Holy Spirit for centuries. One day, every eye will see, every knee will bow, and every tongue will confess the truth of who God is. Or stated another way, "Now I know in part, then I will know fully" (1 Cor. 13:12). For now, though, we will ponder the mystery of the Trinity, and that mystery will draw us deeper into Scripture. Scripture draws and points us deeper into holiness. Deeper holiness leads us to changes in our lives. This is more than deep thinking on a challenging theological truth; this is shaping our very lives by diving daily into the Bible to better know the Father, Son, and Holy Spirit.

As you move day by day through this book, the Word of God will help you better understand the Trinity. You will also become more aware that a Person of the Trinity is with you. The Holy Spirit enables us to grasp Scripture and glimpse the invisible. Each day the living Word of God will challenge you and impact your life. This doctrine is a challenge, but your generation is ready and able to ponder and embrace the spellbinding mystery of the Trinity.

# GETTING STARTED

This devotional contains thirty days of content, broken down into sections. Each day is divided into three elements—discover, delight, and display—to help you grow in your faith.

## discover |

This section helps you examine the passage in light of who God is and determine what it says about your identity in relationship to Him. Included here is the daily Scripture reading and key verses, along with illustrations and commentary to guide you as you learn more about God's Word.

## delight |

In this section, you'll be challenged by questions and activities that help you see how God is alive and active in every detail of His Word and your life.

## display |

Here's where you take action. Display calls you to apply what you've learned through each day's study.

> **Each day also includes a prayer activity at the conclusion of the devotion.**

Throughout the devotional, you'll also find extra items to help you connect with the topic personally, such as Scripture memory verses, additional resources, and interactive articles.

# THE
# FATHER

Judas was leading an armed mob to the Mount of Olives. Jesus was sweating blood as He prayed. From the depths of His anxiety, Jesus taught us about the Father. He called the Father "Abba," revealing the Father's deeply affectionate nature (Mark 14:36). Jesus trusted the Father all the way to the cross and straight into glory. Though the Messiah's path was filled with pain, the Father's perfect will oversaw it all. In this section we will dive into Jesus's life and words about the Father and glimpse the invisible. Let Jesus teach you about the first Person of the Trinity—our loving, gracious, sovereign, unconquerable, and perfectly wise Father.

# BEGIN WITH GOD

READ JOHN 1:1-18.

*No one has ever seen God. The one and only Son, who is himself
God and is at the Father's side—he has revealed him.
—John 1:18*

Think about it—all the things that fight for your attention are all decaying right before your eyes. On top of that, they may not be rooted in truth. Meanwhile, the unseen eternal Truth is calling. Is it time to forsake temporary things and turn your time, eyes, and heart more toward the eternal?

The first six words of the Gospel of John reveal what ancient philosophers sought. They were searching for the origins of logic, reason, and morality, or what they called the *Logos*. God revealed Himself to be the *Logos*, in the person of Jesus. In English, *Logos* is translated as "Word;" that is why John 1:1 states "In the beginning was the Word (*Logos*)"—the origin of all that is true. The origin of all that is true was, is, and always will be Jesus.

Jesus was there in Genesis 1:26 when humanity was created out of an overflow of fellowship between the Father, Son, and Holy Spirit. Our very existence flows from the perfect unity and love they share. It was through Jesus the physical universe was created—including humans who were made in the very image of God. Even though no one has ever seen God the Father with their own eyes, thousands of people saw Jesus. Today we see Jesus through God's Word. If you have seen Jesus, you have seen God, the Father.

# delight |

**Why is it important for us to understand that at creation—including the creation of humanity—all three Persons of the Trinity were present? What does this teach us about God?**

**Describe the security it brings to your heart to know where not only the physical universe ultimately came from, but logic, reason, and morality itself too.**

# display |

As Christians, we confess Jesus as the *Logos*—the ultimate origin of logic and truth—but He is still the *Logos* even for those who do not worship Him. Even Caiaphas, who was plotting to crucify Jesus, was used by God to speak the truth (see John 11:49-53). When you hear something true, whether stated by a Christian or not, you are getting a glimpse of Jesus the *Logos*. Comb through social media, YouTube, or a website you frequently visit and find an example of someone who is not a believer stating something that is true. The reason people who don't know or follow Jesus can speak truth is because all truth belongs to God.

Jesus, I believe You are one with the Father. I believe You are the Word, the *Logos*, alive. I believe You are the unbeatable light shining in our dark world. Jesus, as I am filled with Your Holy Spirit, I confess that You are Lord and repent from my sins.

# ALL PRESENT

## discover |

READ MATTHEW 3:13-17.

*And a voice from heaven said, "This is my beloved Son, with whom I am well-pleased."*
*—Matthew 3:17*

Most coaches have played the sport they coach, drama department directors have experience in the theatre, and it is usually best not to pay for swim lessons from someone who has never swam. It is with full integrity, then, that Jesus calls us to make disciples and baptize them in the name of the Father, Son, and Holy Spirit (see Matt 28:18-20). Jesus never asks us to do something He hasn't already done Himself.

It was at the baptism of Jesus that we first read of the Father's voice audibly speaking from heaven over the Son. Specifically, the Father calls Jesus "beloved" (v. 17). To further confirm their unity, the Father also describes how He feels about the Son. He is well-pleased. This is an epic moment!

The Holy Spirit is revealed in this text as well if you look closely for Him. He is the dove described in verse 16. Note that the Holy Spirit descended, meaning He came from above in heaven. This passage is one of the places in Scripture where we find all three Persons of the Trinity present at the same time—the voice of the Father, the Son being baptized, and the Spirit descending like a dove.

# delight |

**Why was John the Baptist overwhelmed at first at the thought of baptizing Jesus? What did Jesus say to change his mind?**

**Based on verses 16 and 17, how does the Father feel about the Son?**

# display |

Talk to your parents and church leaders about being baptized if you have not already been baptized. Jesus was baptized to "fulfill all righteousness" (v. 15), so we, too, need to be baptized. Baptism does not save us. Rather, we are baptized because we have been saved. Every baptism is a funeral for the sinful self and a symbolic sharing in the resurrection of Jesus (see Rom. 6:4-5)! So the next time you see someone come up from the waters of baptism, you are seeing a reenactment of Jesus's resurrection. Celebrate accordingly!

**God, You are exquisite in Your holiness and majestic in Your power. Thank You, Father, for giving us baptism. Thank You, Jesus, for being baptized. Thank You, Holy Spirit, for blessing Jesus's baptism and blessing my baptism too.**

# REBORN INTO THE LIGHT

## discover |

READ JOHN 3:1-21.

*For God loved the world in this way: He gave his one and only Son, so that everyone who believes in him will not perish but have eternal life.*
*—John 3:16*

Nicodemus met with Jesus at night (see v. 2); he was reluctant to let his fellow Pharisees know he was curious about what Jesus had to say but would later let his light shine (see John 19:39-42). He initially missed the spiritual significance of Jesus's teaching about being born again, too, because it made no sense to him that someone could be reborn physically.

Being physically born a second time wasn't what Jesus was talking about. Light and love have come into our sin-stained world. With our sin, we contribute to the darkness, but Jesus's teachings to Nicodemus in this chapter give us hope that we may be spiritually reborn into the light—as it seems Nicodemus eventually was too.

This is Jesus teaching about the love of the Father and the Spirit making it possible for sinful people like us to be born all over again. We were born into a sinful nature, but because of the ultimate act of love, we may have eternal life (see vv. 15-16). By default, we are rightly condemned, but by the Father's love, we can be reborn into the light and let the world see what He has accomplished through us (see v. 21).

# delight |

**How would you coach Nicodemus to better understand Jesus's teaching about being born again?**

**Describe below how it makes you feel to know that we have the opportunity to have life because of the love of the Father revealed through what Jesus did on the cross.**

# display |

According to Ephesians 2:10, God has prepared ahead of time good works for us to do. God has prepared opportunities for you to share the eternal life-giving message of John 3:1-21. So, share this with someone this week, whether online or in person. Instead of preparing and rehearsing a speech, study the passage once more so that, carried along by the unseen wind of the Spirit, you can speak genuinely from your heart in a way that is tailored for the heart of your listener. Someone out there needs to hear these words this week.

God, I was hiding my sin in the dark, but You saw me and loved me right where I was. You called me into the light and I was reborn when I believed in Your Son Jesus. Holy Spirit of God, anoint me to invite others into this glorious light.

# CHECK YOUR WORRIES

## discover |

READ MATTHEW 6:25-34.

*"Consider the birds of the sky: They don't sow or reap or gather into barns, yet
your heavenly Father feeds them. Aren't you worth more than they?"*
*—Matthew 6:26*

Do you have any idea how much you are worth to God? Imagine the
most beautiful sunset in the history of the Grand Canyon. Add in the
most majestic bald eagles in the history of their species. Then hit play
on the most exquisite soundtrack ever composed. Put it all together
and you still have something of less value than you.

The verses you read today are the Son of God speaking on behalf of
the Father, officially declaring your value of higher worth than all of
creation. Invite the Spirit to press these words upon your heart until you
believe them. Take seriously that this is Jesus describing the Father and
how He feels about you!

God takes care of His creation. He has taken care of you and will
continue to do so. Choosing to give in to or resist the temptation to
worry is a matter of either believing Jesus in Matthew 6:25-34 or not.
These Spirit-inspired words lift our hearts from petty concerns like
clothing and point our eyes toward God's eternal kingdom. When we
focus on Him, everything else falls into place (see v. 33).

# delight |

**What shifts in your heart when you see how plain your needs are to Jesus?**

**Jesus brought this profound teaching to a clear and simple take-away in verse 34. What was it?**

# display |

List your worries in bullet-point fashion and be brutally honest as you do. Hold nothing back and plow through that self-conscious feeling that someone might read what you wrote: this is between you and God. Now, next to each worry, write the words, *"An opportunity to trust Jesus."* Each of these items is fully within the sovereignty (authority) of God to handle, and each of these items has distracted you from the eternal mission of God's kingdom and directed your valuable attention to something temporary. At the bottom of your list, write in gigantic letters, "SEEK GOD FIRST!"

God, I am checking my bags. I am offloading these worries that I was never meant to bear. Forgive me for not trusting in You. Help me to grasp just how extravagant Your love is for me. I hereby lift my eyes to seek You and Your kingdom first.

# ONE

## discover |

READ JOHN 10:22-39.

*"I and the Father are one."*
*—John 10:30*

When someone shows up and starts claiming to be God, we who live after the resurrection of Jesus know it's a lie. But what about Old Testament believers who were waiting for the Messiah? Old Testament believers saw centuries come and go with God's promises for the coming Christ yet to be fulfilled, but they believed He would come eventually.

When the day finally came and Jesus was standing before the Jewish leaders, their corporate response was to have Him killed. Their statement in verse 24, "If you are the Messiah, tell us plainly," was especially ridiculous when some of their group had already tried to kill Jesus in John 8.

Jesus's words in verses 34-36 are some of the most difficult to understand in all of His teachings. He was quoting Psalm 82:6 to show that His divine claim had a scriptural basis. Jesus's point was that, as His miraculous works proved, He was One with God the Father and His claim was founded upon the very law His critics clung to. In the face of fierce opposition, Jesus was righteously steadfast in His claim that He and the Father are One.

# delight |

Denying that Jesus was One with the Father is the same as accusing Him of lying. How do people in our time accuse Jesus of lying?

Describe what happens in your heart when you read Jesus's words in verse 28. What does Jesus mean by them?

# display |

Store up Jesus's words in your heart, calling upon them when the enemy attacks your security in your salvation. Memorize John 10:28-30 not just for your sake but to comfort a Christian friend when the enemy attacks them as well: "I give them eternal life, and they will never perish. No one will snatch them out of my hand. My Father, who has given them to me, is greater than all. No one is able to snatch them out of the Father's hand. I and the Father are one."

God, You are greater than all. I know Your Holy Spirit is in my heart. Father, I believe that You raised Your Son from the dead (see Rom. 10:9). Nothing can take me from Your hands. I will do as Jesus did: proclaim my unity with You despite opposition.

# REVELATION AND REJECTION

## discover |

READ LUKE 10:1-24.

*"All things have been entrusted to me by my Father. No one knows
who the Son is except the Father, and who the Father is except the
Son, and anyone to whom the Son desires to reveal him."*
*—Luke 10:22*

Even if your skeptical friends saw a miracle before their very eyes, they
still might not believe that God is real and that Jesus is who they need
to place their faith in. Look at today's reading for proof. Miracles were
performed. Demons were exorcised. Even still, not everyone believed.
This has been the case for thousands of years. Even people who saw
the miracles of Jesus directly did not automatically believe. In fact, it
was partly because of Jesus's miracles that His earthly enemies wanted
Him crucified.

Jesus gave authority to these seventy-two people to reveal the truth
to the outlying cities. When confronted with miraculous proof of the
gospel, the people of some towns rejected the message. Many of
these people used the desire to see proof or evidence from Jesus as an
excuse. The hard reality is that they didn't really want to believe. They
already had more than enough proof in creation alone but just wanted
to continue in sin (see Rom. 1).

The burden of proof is not on your shoulders when you share about
Jesus. Rather, the opportunity for faith is on your hearers. While not
everyone will receive the good news that Jesus is One with the Father,
not everyone rejects God either, so be faithful to share.

# delight |

**Jesus knowingly sent the seventy-two into harm's way (see v. 3). What does this reveal about God's will for your life?**

**The Father, the Son, and the Holy Spirit are all beautifully at work together in verses 21 and 22. Describe the role each Person of the Trinity plays in the moment someone is saved based on these verses.**

# display |

Today, we will ask God for the same position of privilege that was lavished on the disciples in verses 23 and 24. We will ask God to let us watch Him work in someone's life today and seize the opportunity to share the gospel when He opens the opportunity. Whether they confess Jesus as Lord (see Rom. 10:9) by the power of the Holy Spirit (see 1 Cor. 12:3), or reject Him, we have walked in faithfulness. Pray that the Son reveals Himself to someone today, then share the gospel using John 3:16 and watch the Spirit work.

**Sovereign God, take over my plans for today. I pray that the Son would reveal the Father to someone I encounter, and I hereby commit to share John 3:16 when You open the door. Whatever comes next, I cannot wait to see You at work, Jesus.**

MEMORY VERSE
**JOHN 10:28-30**

"I GIVE THEM ETERNAL LIFE, AND THEY WILL NEVER PERISH. NO ONE WILL SNATCH THEM OUT OF MY HAND. MY FATHER, WHO HAS GIVEN THEM TO ME, IS GREATER THAN ALL. NO ONE IS ABLE TO SNATCH THEM OUT OF THE FATHER'S HAND. I AND THE FATHER ARE ONE."

# THE FAITHFUL FATHER

## discover |

READ LUKE 15:11-32.

*So he got up and went to his father. But while the son was still a
long way off, his father saw him and was filled with compassion. He
ran, threw his arms around his neck, and kissed him.*
*—Luke 15:20*

There are deep layers to this parable. On one level, Jesus gave a picture
of the Father's heart toward His Old Testament chosen nation of Israel and
toward the Gentiles (non-Jewish people). On another level, Jesus showed
how God the Father feels about the wayward who repent from sin and come
home to Him. Notice how the son did not finish the speech he prepared for
his father. According to verse 19, he was going to ask to be hired on as a
worker, but the father interrupted his speech in verse 21 so that he did not
get to it. Instead, he was welcomed home by his compassionate, faithful,
and loving father; no labor necessary.

This parable could also be called "The Faithful Father" because, while it
echoes what we already know to be true about our sinful selves, it reveals
what we could not see on the other side of the relationship. When we
act like the prodigal son, we often imagine the worst about our heavenly
Father's heart toward us. Then, with this parable, the Son revealed the
compassionate Father who has been faithfully waiting for our homecoming
all along.

# delight

Did the lost son deserve this compassion? For that matter, did the son who stayed home earn anything he had? Switch the roles of the sons to modern believers, then explain.

When you envision God the Father's face toward you at your worst moments, what do you see? Are there any adjustments to make in your perception of the Father based on today's verses?

# display |

Come running home to your heavenly Father if you have been running astray in some area of your life. Search your heart for any plans you have to try to earn His love back and cast them aside. Sprint into the open arms of the faithful Father and receive His embrace. Believe and know based on the very words of Jesus that He loves you despite every last one of your sins. Fold your arms into an embrace as you pray this prayer:

Thank You, Father. Thank You. Thank You for Your endless grace. You throw my sins as far as the east is from the west time and time again (see Ps. 103:12). You throw Your arms around my rebellious soul when I come home, watching me return from afar.

# DOWN A NOTCH

## discover |

READ MATTHEW 23:8-12.

*"Do not call anyone on earth your father, because you*
*have one Father, who is in heaven. "*
*—Matthew 23:9*

This was more than a social media take-down or a "hot take" on a
TV show. It was a desperately needed proclamation of justice for the
spiritually oppressed from Jesus. For the first years of Jesus's ministry,
He would disappear into the crowds after laying down the law and
even encouraged the people He had miraculously healed to keep quiet
about it because His time had not yet come. However, at this point,
knowing that the cross was near, Jesus began calling the Pharisees out
and revealing that they were the "bad guys" in His parables for the last
three years (see Matt. 21:45).

This passage is a glimpse into Jesus's barrage of truths taking the
Pharisees down a notch to show them that, though they thought
themselves to be spiritually elite, they were just as needy for a Savior
as the people they had oppressed with burdensome, made-up laws.
Jesus's words have a unifying effect. We collectively have one Teacher,
Father, Instructor, and Messiah. We are all under God's authority, and
none of us is more inherently righteous than anyone else. We were all
born sinful. The utterly amazing news is that we have a gracious Father
who loves us and longs for us to come to Him through Jesus.

*Three-In-One*

# delight |

Should we not refer to our biological or adoptive fathers as "father" because of verse 9, or was Jesus talking about spiritual leaders who elevate themselves over others? Explain.

How do verses 11 and 12 reframe the common practice on social media of painting ourselves in a glamorous and even fake light?

# display |

It is deeply satisfying to see prideful people taken down a notch the way Jesus took down the Pharisees. This passage becomes all the more real, though, when we press it to our own hearts. Hold Jesus's words up like a mirror. Journal an honest inventory of your behavior. Have you been exalting yourself? If you use social media, skim your recent posts and spot the humble brags and posts secretly or even overtly motivated by pride. Replay recent conversations and analyze your own motives, searching for self-exaltation. Let verses 11 and 12 serve as God's wrecking ball. Then let the Holy Spirit rebuild you with huge cinder blocks of grace instead of pride.

God, I lift up the spiritual leaders in my life. Please protect them from the same spirit of pride that overtook the Pharisees. Let their humility come from a soft yet pervasive awareness of Your grace for sinners like us. Protect me from pride too, God. Forgive me for exalting myself in the past.

# RADICAL OBEDIENCE

## discover |

READ JOHN 14:27-31.

*"On the contrary, so that the world may know that I love*
*the Father, I do as the Father commanded me."*
*—John 14:31a*

The disciples had no idea what was coming, but Jesus did. Jesus had told them about His approaching death and resurrection, but the words did not sink in. As Jesus spoke these words of peace to His disciples, Judas was en route with Roman troops to arrest Jesus. He knew exactly what was about to happen. His disciples were clueless.

The crucifixion was not the will of Satan (see v. 30). The Father was in control the entire time, and Jesus was acting in obedience to Him (see v. 31). The love of the Son for the Father was about to be on dramatic display, but Jesus knew the disciples would not understand in the coming trauma, so He gave them perfect words of peace (see v. 27). He told them this ahead of time so that they would believe when it all went down (see v. 29), then literally got up and brought them closer to a place where He secretly knew He would be arrested (see v. 31). He was telling them not to let their hearts be troubled while knowingly taking them into harm's way. Philippians 2:5-11 gives us another divine glimpse into the Son's selfless motives as He obeyed the Father all the way to the cross.

# delight |

Why do you believe Jesus used the word "let" specifically when instructing His disciples, *"Don't let your heart be troubled or fearful,"* in verse 27?

In verse 28, Jesus told the disciples that He would be with them again after His departure, but the disciples still scattered after the crucifixion. Why do you think the disciples forgot about this after the cross?

# display |

The peace that the world gives is cheap and ridiculously fragile. Things can appear to be going great, only to collapse into chaos in an instant. It is peace that is given and then taken away. True peace is far more than just the absence of difficulty. The peace that Jesus gives withstands tragedy. Prayerfully take this peace upon your heart. Talk to God about it until you can say with full integrity: "*I will not let my heart be troubled or fearful.*" Make this the anthem of your heart because difficulty is approaching if it is not here already.

Jesus, You obeyed the Father to the cross. I will obey through my own trials, knowing with gratitude that they are nothing compared to what You endured. I will not let my heart be troubled or fearful. I will take the peace that Jesus offers instead of the world's "peace."

# ABBA, FATHER

## discover |

READ MARK 14:32-42.

*And he said, "Abba, Father! All things are possible for you. Take this cup*
*away from me. Nevertheless, not what I will, but what you will."*
*—Mark 14:36*

Jesus's words in verse 42 were interrupted by the arrival of Judas
accompanied by a mob with swords and clubs (see Mark 14:43). This
passage describes the disciples' final minutes of semi-blissful ignorance.
They were literally napping while an armed mob approached them
in the garden of Gethsemane. Meanwhile, the Son was talking to the
Father, and the insights we glean from Jesus's prayer are astounding.

It's important to remember that Jesus was fully God and fully human.
Everything that was human about Jesus was sweating blood in dread
for the approaching cross (see Luke 22:44), yet Jesus knew that it had
to come to pass. Jesus referred to what He knew would be the most
brutal execution in history as a "cup" which He alone could drink. He
absolutely did not want this cup, but He knew it was better by far to
obey the Father's will and make atonement for the sins of all who
believe in Him across time. This is not a war of the wills between Father
and Son, but an expression of human despair from God the Son to God
the Father. The word He used to address the Father in verse 36, *Abba*,
carries deep affection and intimacy. Behold the deep love between the
Father and Son in the time of the Son's greatest imaginable anxiety.
Even though the Son had to drink the cup, the Father's love for Him
never wavered. His love never wavers for us either, as evidenced by
Jesus having to drink the cup.

# delight |

As Jesus's humanity struggled in dreadful anticipation for the cross to come, what human struggle were the disciples exhibiting while trying to pray for Jesus in verses 37-40?

What do you believe Jesus meant when He prayed, *"Take this cup from me,"* in verse 36? How does His resolution to do the Father's will despite it all inspire you?

# display |

Drink deeply from the cup the Father has given you. Jesus drank His, and none of our cups contain a fraction of what Jesus consumed on our behalf. Drink deeply from the cup without thought of jealousy over the contents of someone else's cup. You have been called to this ministry. They have been called to theirs. Jesus drank His, and now we must drink ours. Whoever told you that following Jesus meant receiving only good things either lied to you or never read Mark 14. Jesus drank the cup we could not. Following Jesus, we will drink the cups we have been given, but we will always know the Father loves us and the Spirit is with us.

Jesus, thank You for drinking the cup given to You by the Father. You called me to this time and place for a reason. I will not worry about what is in the cups of my friends. You have given me this cup, and I will drink it—pain and all.

# THE
# SON

Take His own words for it. Everything you need to know about Jesus is in Scripture, ready to be unveiled by the Holy Spirit. Encounter Jesus through His own words. Join Him in His teachings. Envision Him by His friend Lazarus's tomb. Watch through Scripture as He ministers to a woman in public humiliation. We have glimpsed the invisible Father through the Son's words. Now, we will look to the Son Himself.

## DAY 11

# FREE BREAD!

## discover |

READ JOHN 6:22-59.

*"I am the bread of life," Jesus told them. "No one who comes to me will ever be hungry, and no one who believes in me will ever be thirsty again."*
*—John 6:35*

It is ironic that atheists would quote verse 53, citing it as a reason for their disbelief. That was part of its purpose. After Jesus gave this difficult teaching, the huge crowd of thousands who were looking for a free meal (see v. 26) dispersed, and only His disciples remained (see John 6:60-69). It would not be until Jesus gave the elements of the Passover meal the night leading up to His crucifixion, equating His body with the bread and His blood with the cup, that they would see what this teaching foreshadowed.

Jesus had already defied physics right before the insatiable crowd's eyes to feed them, yet they had the gall to ask, "What sign, then, are you going to do so that we may see and believe you?" (v. 30). They missed the eternal significance of the miracle. Jesus is the Bread of Life who comes from heaven, whose provisions we could never earn, and whose grace never runs out for those who believe in Him. If only they had believed fully, rather than sticking around as long as the free food held up, they would have understood why Jesus performed the miracles in the first place. The limitless and miraculous bread was a heavenly metaphor representing Jesus Himself.

*Lifeway Students | Devotions*     42

delight |

Review verses 22-24 to see the lengths to which this miraculously fed crowd went to follow Jesus, then describe their true motives according to verse 26.

Jesus told them everything they needed to know about Him and how to be saved between verses 26 and 31. What is the crucial teaching the miracle-hungry crowd missed?

# display |

Not to bum you out, but everyone who was miraculously healed, brought back to life, or fed in the Bible eventually died. The miracle itself was not enough. The reason for the miracle was to point people's eyes heavenward. So, ask yourself honestly if you have focused too much on what Jesus can give you and missed Jesus Himself in the process. This is what the miracle-hungry crowd walking away from the Bread of Life Himself did. If the Spirit convicts you of this, repent today.

Jesus, the manna that fell from heaven to miraculously feed the Israelites in Exodus 16 was just a glimpse into the future, foreshadowing You. Forgive me for ways in which I, like the crowd, have looked past You to fixate on what You can give me. I need You more than anything.

## DAY 12

# LIGHT OF THE WORLD

## discover |

READ JOHN 8:12-21.

*Jesus spoke to them again: "I am the light of the world. Anyone who follows
me will never walk in the darkness but will have the light of life."*
*—John 8:12*

Jesus made seven "I am" statements in the book of John, and this is
the second one of them. Each time Jesus made an "I am" statement,
He was directly aligning Himself with the Father who called Himself "I
AM" in Exodus 3:14. In today's verses, Jesus said to His listeners, "I am
the light of the world" (v. 12).

The law to which Jesus referred in verse 17 is Deuteronomy 19:15,
establishing that one must have at least one other credible witness
in order for his claim to be considered true. In today's verses, Jesus
brought the ultimate Witness to attest to the truthfulness of His
claims about Himself. Not that Jesus needed to prove Himself to the
hypocritical Pharisees, but the Witness Jesus brought was none other
than God the Father. How do you dispute that? Because the Pharisees
did not know the Father, they did not respect Jesus's authority, and the
same is true for those who deny Jesus today.

*Three-In-One*

# delight |

How did Jesus proclaim His alignment with the Father in verse 19?

We cannot be saved if we deny that Jesus is the Son of God (v. 21). Was Jesus being overly harsh or righteously truthful when He proclaimed this in verse 21? Why?

# display |

Our world is dark because we have denied Jesus as the *Logos* (see Day 1) and the light of the world, choosing instead to be our own gauges for individual senses of truth. Our eyes see on social media and the news what happens when we live by our own fluctuating and selfishly motivated senses of truth. The ultimate foundation for truth is Jesus, the Light of the world whose testimony is verified by the Father Himself. We must lay down individual "truth" for the Truth Himself—Jesus, the Light of the world.

Identify one way you have exchanged real truth for a personal truth that does not hold to God's Word. Ask God to help you fight against the urge to exchange the real for something fake.

**Jesus, You are the Bread of Life and the light of the world. I hereby lay my sense of individual truth at Your feet. Your testimony is verified by the Father, and I trust You more than I trust my sinful self. Illuminate my steps, Jesus.**

# TEACHER'S PETS

## discover |

READ JOHN 8:31-47.

*"So if the Son sets you free, you really will be free."*
*—John 8:36*

Isaiah prophesied that Jesus's earthly enemies would listen but not understand and look but not perceive (see Isa. 6:9-10), and this prophecy was fulfilled in part through the events of today's verses. Like evil versions of teacher's pets who write their own extra credit assignments and look down on others for not doing the same, they actually loved the rigorous rule-following of the Old Testament so much that they added to God's commands. They were enslaved to their own legalism and resented Jesus's invitation to freedom (see v. 32).

When you read the entire Gospel of John, you will notice that Jesus's words in verse 37 went uncontested for the first time. They were no longer denying their intent to kill Him. In fact, they would pick up rocks to stone Him by the time this conversation came to an end.

In verse 41, Jesus referred to them as children of the devil! Their response could have been a slight against Jesus, suggesting they did not believe Mary was a virgin. They once again appealed to their ethnicity as Jews as though it put them above Jesus's teachings. Abraham's greatest hope was standing right in front of them, but they could not see Him. Isaiah was right.

**delight** |

**Why is verse 45 profound in a world wherein truth statements are becoming increasingly offensive?**

**What parallels do you see between the Pharisee's refusal to even consider Jesus on His own terms and modern culture's tendency to demote Jesus to a mere teacher?**

# display |

The Old Testament Law, since the resurrection of Jesus, serves as the measure by which we become aware of sin (see Rom. 3:20). The only command we are given in the New Testament is to love (see John 13:34,35). The legalism of the Pharisees can take root in modern Christians' hearts too, causing us to take pride in our obedience to commands that Jesus did not give us.

Ask the Holy Spirit to guide you as you examine your heart. Have you allowed unbiblical commands and laws not found in the Bible to take root? Relish in Jesus's proclamation of freedom instead.

> **Jesus, I believe You. You set us absolutely free from sin. You fulfilled the Law. By Your Spirit, show me any tendencies within me to obligate myself to laws that You did not issue. Replace them with Your freedom. Protect me from the arrogance of the Pharisees.**

# TIME MACHINE

## discover |

READ JOHN 8:48-59.

*Jesus said to them, "Truly I tell you, before Abraham was, I am."*
*—John 8:58*

In verse 48 you can see the heart behind the Pharisees' crazy question right away. "Aren't we right?" isn't a genuine request for an answer; it's a desire to be told, "You're right." Not only did Jesus obviously not have a demon inside of Him, but He was born in Bethlehem, so He wasn't a Samaritan either.

Because Jesus is the *Logos*, having existed from before the beginning, His words in verse 58 that threw the Pharisees into a murderous rage are absolutely true. If you had a time machine and could step into the text at verse 59 and ask the Pharisees what they were thinking, they would likely quote Deuteronomy 13:6-11 and Leviticus 24:16, which instructed the Jews to stone those who committed idolatry and claimed to be God. But there are two colossal problems. For one, this *was* the Son of God. Two, Deuteronomy 17:2-7 required that they first gather the testimonies of two or three witnesses and have a formal trial. The Pharisees in these verses skipped that step and jumped straight to capital punishment by way of a murderous mob. These men prided themselves on their adherence to the law but violated it as they closed in on Jesus for stating the truth of who He is.

# delight |

**Why was it better for God to glorify Jesus than for Him to bring glory to Himself during His time on earth?**

**How is Jesus's proclamation in verse 58 parallel to what God the Father said about Himself to Moses in Exodus 3:14?**

# display |

Notice how Jesus approached the flawed questions of the Pharisees. They began by asking the Son of God if He had a demon. Jesus denied it. They responded, "Now we know you have a demon," in verse 52. They labeled Him, then interpreted His denial as proof of the label. Learn to, like Jesus, spot questions that are not honest or neutral and keep your cool when they are asked. Like Jesus, know whose you are, see through the question, and rest in the Father.

Jesus, You existed before a single atom of the universe was formed. You were One with the Father long before Abraham existed. The Father attests to Your glory and so will I. Praise You, Jesus.

# THE GATE

## discover |

READ JOHN 10:1-10.

*"I am the gate. If anyone enters by me, he will be saved and will come in and go out and find pasture. A thief comes only to steal and kill and destroy. I have come so that they may have life and have it in abundance."*
*—John 10:9-10*

The devil was at work through the Pharisees, Sadducees, and teachers of the law who opposed Jesus at every turn. The thief in Jesus's parable was the devil, but he used the corrupt religious leadership to carry out his work. The outcome when the enemy attacks is destruction and ultimately death. The outcome of the Pharisees' legalistic oppression was thievery, destruction, and death as this group of corrupt leaders led people astray and saw to it that Jesus was crucified.

In verse 10, take note of the stark contrast between the effect of the enemy and the effect of Jesus. It is not just that the sheep who follow the Good Shepherd have life—Jesus said that they may have life in abundance (see v. 10)! This abundance comes from who He is. Continuing His echoes of the Father's "I AM" proclamation, Jesus called Himself both the gate for the sheep (see v. 7) and the good shepherd (vv. 11,14). Here is the amazing news: if you are a Christian, you are one of Jesus's sheep. You have a Good Shepherd. You have a way to come into grace, a familiar voice to follow, and a protector in Him.

# delight |

Notice Jesus said He is "the" gate and not 'a' gate. What is the difference between Jesus being "the" gate versus 'a' gate and why is that important?

What does the word "abundance" in verse 10 reveal about the heart of the Good Shepherd toward His sheep?

*Three-In-One*

# display |

Give credit where it is due. Whatever has been stolen, God did not steal it; the enemy did. Whatever has been maliciously killed, God did not kill it; the enemy did. Whatever has been meaninglessly or spitefully destroyed, God did not destroy it; the enemy did. It is the scandal of the millennia that God would be blamed for what the enemy has done. If you have accused God of wrongdoing, repent of that before Him today and proclaim your trust in Him as the Good Shepherd. Plant your heart upon John 10:10, trusting in His coming justice on the thief.

Jesus, You spoke these incredible words to Your people who were enslaved by spiritual thieves and robbers. I see You in Your words, Jesus. You are my gate, my only way to salvation. You are my Shepherd, and You are good. I relish in the abundant life you give me!

# HEROIC SHEPHERD

## discover |

READ JOHN 10:11-21.

*"I am the good shepherd. The good shepherd lays down his life for the sheep."*
*—John 10:11*

When people are willing to lay their lives down for the well-being of others, we call them heroes. It is why so many people—regardless of where they stand politically—admire members of our military. Many brave people have said, "I will lay down my life," but only One has ever said, "I have the right to lay it down, and I have the right to take it up again." That One is Jesus, our Good Shepherd.

When Jesus called Himself our Good Shepherd right after healing a man who was born blind, the crowd wasn't quite sure what to think. Some thought He was crazy. Others wondered (again) if maybe He was demon-possessed. But Jesus wasn't there for division; He was there for unity. To invite not just Jews but all people into His kingdom. And that invitation would come at a very high price.

Jesus is no ordinary shepherd. He is willing to lay down His life for His sheep. He is not a distant and disconnected God. Rather, He speaks to us through His Word and by His Spirit. He is speaking right now to you! He knows you (see v. 14). Read today's verses again and listen to Him.

# delight |

**Contrast verses 12 and 13 with what Jesus did on the cross. How does this contrast reveal the trustworthiness of Jesus?**

**According to Jesus's own words, what is one reason the Father loves Him?**

# display |

Verse 16 is not Jesus's way of saying that all people, regardless of their beliefs, will be saved one day. He was actually making a radical racial statement for His context. He was saying that Gentiles could be the people of God as well as Jews who had been known as God's chosen people. The tensions that existed between Jews and Gentiles in Jesus's context were fiery. Jesus's words in verse 16 were living water to extinguish the flames of hatred. This ministry of reconciliation came at the ultimate cost—Jesus's life—and was sealed by the ultimate victory—Jesus's resurrection (see v. 18). The result is two flocks becoming one, and we all have one Shepherd. This truth lives today. Jesus is for everyone, not just people who look like you or speak your language or live in neighborhoods like yours. The Good Shepherd is for everyone.

Name some people in your church, school, or community who are different from you. Beneath the list, write out "Jesus is for him or her too." Then, highlight the names of people you know who don't know Jesus. Ask God to give you the opportunity to share with him or her the good news of Jesus.

Jesus, You know my flaws and love me still. It is the honor of my life to hear Your voice through Your words and know it is the voice of my heroic Shepherd who laid down His life for His sheep of many pastures and then took it back up again.

MEMORY VERSE
**John 14:6-7**

Jesus told him, "I am the way, the truth, and the life. No one comes to the Father except through me. If you know me, you will also know my Father. From now on you do know him and have seen him."

# LAZARUS'S FIRST FUNERAL

## discover |

READ JOHN 11:17-44.

*Jesus said to her, "I am the resurrection and the life. The one who believes in me, even if he dies, will live."*
*—John 11:25*

This mind-blowing miracle is the fifth of Jesus's seven "I am" statements in the Gospel of John. "I am the resurrection and the life" (v. 25). Because Jesus claimed to embody resurrection itself, it stands to reason that He would have the power to resurrect Lazarus. This miracle was proof. It was also foreshadowing. In our passage yesterday, Jesus claimed to have the right to take His own life back up again after laying it down. Indeed, the resurrection and the life Himself would be crucified and resurrected.

Look closely at Martha in verses 20-27 and remember this critical fact: she came to these remarkably faith-filled conclusions without a complete New Testament to read. The Book of Revelation would not even be written until decades after the events of today's verses, yet Martha knew about the coming resurrection of all who are God's. The Mary named in this text is not Jesus's earthly mother but Lazarus and Martha's sister—all dear friends of Jesus. Both Martha and Mary said the same things to Jesus: "Lord, if you had been here, my brother would not have died!" (vv. 21,32). However, Jesus met each sister where she was at emotionally and chose simply to ask where they had put Lazarus and weep with them . . . but not for long.

# delight |

Who do you relate to more—Martha, the level-headed, inquisitive sister? Or Mary, the more emotional, wear-your-heart-on-your-sleeve sister? How can God use the way you're wired for His glory?

If Jesus had come immediately, He could have healed Lazarus and saved this family from the drama of the situation. Why was it important that Jesus waited until after Lazarus died to come see them? (Hint: see John 11:41-42.)

# display |

This is not a doomsday prophecy but more a biblical statement about your current reality on this side of heaven: hardship is on the horizon. Jesus knew full well that Lazarus was dying, yet He wept nonetheless. He could have prevented it, but He did not. He set the stage to miraculously come through in this story. So when, not if, hardship arrives, make your mind up right now before you get up that you will face it with the faith of Martha. Know that Jesus is the resurrection and the life amidst the coming hardship.

Jesus, You are the resurrection and the life. You proved it with tears in Your eyes by the tomb of Your friend Lazarus. When You allow me to face hardship, I will trust in You. In the face of death itself, I will know that You are good.

# "THE" DEFINITE ARTICLE

## discover |

READ JOHN 14:1-7.

*Jesus told him, "I am the way, the truth, and the life. No one comes to the Father except through me. If you know me, you will also know my Father. From now on you do know him and have seen him."*
*—John 14:6-7*

Did you see that pesky word "let" again when it comes to our hearts being troubled? Read verse 1 again. We have a choice. It is easier by far to give way to despair. It is incredibly hard to exercise faith in settings like this passage's original context. The cross was coming, and Jesus's disciples were perplexed by His warning to them that He was about to go somewhere they could not follow. They had been following Him for three years and wanted to know the way.

Jesus's answer to Thomas's heartwrenching question in verse 5 provides one of the clearest claims Jesus made to the truth in all of Scripture. Think back to English class: the word "the" is called the "definite article," and Jesus used it three times in the singular form. He did not claim to be "a way," or "a truth," or "a life." There is no way aside from Jesus to get to the Father. There is no other truth but Jesus. There is no life found in anyone aside from Jesus. There are not multiple ways to heaven. There is one—through Jesus.

# delight |

**What is the one way we can know God the Father? What verse or verses prove your answer?**

**According to verses 2 and 3, where was Jesus going and what was He going to do? Why is this important?**

# display |

Whether in person or online, let Jesus have a seat at the table the next time you are in proximity to a discussion on the nature of truth. When you hear someone say words like "your truth" or "my truth," listen intently for the words the Holy Spirit will give you to introduce the group to Jesus's words in this text. There is no "your truth." There is only Jesus. This is not intellectual arrogance: it is reading comprehension, and Jesus did not lie.

Jesus, I believe You at Your very own words. You are the only way to the Father. You are the truth personified. You are the only life, and there is no life outside of You. Help me to follow You wherever You lead.

# REMAIN

## discover |

READ JOHN 15:1-8.

*"I am the vine; you are the branches. The one who remains in me and I in*
*him produces much fruit, because you can do nothing without me."*
*—John 15:5*

Nothing. We can do nothing apart from Jesus (see v. 5). As we faithfully remain (see vv. 4-7) in close fellowship with Jesus through both droughts and harvests, we start to do God's will instead of our own. Note Jesus's very particular and deliberately repeated word choice. He said "remain" seven times in just four verses! God's will is not something we periodically visit. It is where we stay, where we remain. With your sturdy roots planted deep in the soil of God's will, the things you desire will change. As your desires change from what you want to what God wants, what you pray for changes to what God wants and every single prayer that aligns with the will of God gets a big booming "yes" from heaven.

The process Jesus described is painful, though. This parable describes both God the Gardener trimming away fruitless investments of time and resources in a Christian's life and God casting away the fruitless false believers (see v. 6). We know we are connected to the vine when we do the will of God and bear fruit (see Matt. 7:21). But the only way to bear fruit is to remain. We can't go and do our own thing and expect to be fruitful followers of Jesus.

**delight** |

What habits in your life help you to remain in Jesus?

Think of a time when you did your own thing. Then contrast that to a time when you remained in Jesus and bore fruit. What are differences between those two experiences?

# display |

Say "yes" to God as He cuts away the things in your life that do not bear fruit so that you can bear much fruit (see v. 5) and glorify the Father (see vv. 2,8). Be brave! It is painful to surrender these precious yet fruitless branches to God, but the result is awesome. Bear fruit that is eternally significant, remain in Christ all the days of your life, and watch your prayers in accordance with God's will get answered like crazy (see v.7). Say "yes" to God.

Remove from my schedule, my priorities, and my emotional investments the practices that bear zero fruit for You, God. Prune my life by cutting away even things that do not seem that bad, but do not produce spiritual results. I want to bear not just occasional fruit, but much fruit.

**DAY 20**

# INCOMING!

## discover |

READ MATTHEW 24:36-44.

*"Now concerning that day and hour no one knows—neither the angels of heaven nor the Son—except the Father alone."*
*—Matthew 24:36*

Jesus could come back before you finish reading this sentence. He could come back before you finish reading this . . . one. Okay, you get the picture. Since you are still reading, then evidently we have all yet to see the time that only the Father knows. This is a pivotal and rare teaching from the Scripture from which we draw our understanding of the Trinity. This is the only place in Scripture where Jesus said the Father knows something He does not. What's beautiful about this is it reaffirms the faith the Son has in the Father and the love they share.

The reference Jesus was making in verses 37-39 was the hard-partying people of Noah's day who were swept up in the flood. God did what He said He would do in those days. He will do this too. Because no one knows when the return of Jesus will be but the Father, we must constantly be in a state of repentance and doing God's will.

When you see someone make a prediction about the timing of the second coming of Jesus, remember HIs words in today's verses and live as if it could be today.

# delight |

Based on verses 40-44, what do you think would happen if everyone knew the exact time Jesus would return?

Jesus does not want us to live in fear of His return but in expectant preparation. How can you live expectantly for the return of Jesus instead of fearfully?

# display |

With a sense of urgency brought upon your heart by the Holy Spirit's work through this passage, let your faith be known and share the gospel with someone this week. We do not know the time or the hour, so we do not know how much time we have. If you have been procrastinating sharing your faith, let this passage be the spur that gets you to make a move in accordance with the Holy Spirit's will. You do not know if the next conversation you have with your friends could be your last, so make it count eternally.

> Jesus, now that You have cut out of my life the things that do not bear fruit, replace them with relationships, hobbies, and endeavors that allow me to bear spiritual fruit while I still can on this earth. Father, you alone know the time. Use me to the absolute most as Your return grows nearer and nearer.

# THE HOLY SPIRIT

In the opening chapter of Acts, Jesus ascended to heaven. He said it was better for Him to ascend because had He not ascended to heaven, the Holy Spirit would not come down (see John 16:7). God's direct presence on the earth in Eden was the direct presence of the Father Himself. His direct presence on the earth in Jesus's day was Jesus Himself. Today, the direct presence of God on the earth is the Holy Spirit Himself.

# OVERSHADOWED

## discover |

READ LUKE 1:26-38.

*The angel replied to her, "The Holy Spirit will come upon you, and the power of the Most High will overshadow you. Therefore, the holy one to be born will be called the Son of God." —Luke 1:35*

In ancient mythology there are stories of gods fathering children through mortal women. There are even myths of virgin births. But there is absolutely nothing in the whole of literature that compares to this account from the Word of God. Why? Because those are stories. This is history. Look back at the word "overshadow" in verse 35. This was the Holy Spirit doing something that is impossible. Like the angel told Mary—a beloved servant of extraordinary faith—with God, nothing is impossible (see v. 37).

About seven centuries before Jesus was born, the same Holy Spirit inspired Isaiah to write a beautiful prophecy. "Therefore, the Lord himself will give you a sign: See, the virgin will conceive, have a son, and name him Immanuel" (Isa. 7:14). How could Isaiah have known what would happen? Once again, God does the impossible.

Centuries before Isaiah, at the very beginning of humanity, God the Father foretold that the offspring of woman would conquer the serpent (see Gen. 3:15). The conception of the Son was a miracle brought by the Holy Spirit according to the prophesied will of God the Father. With God, nothing is ever impossible!

# delight

**Read verse 38 again. Is there something happening in your life right now where you need to respond like Mary?**

**What do verses 34 and 35 tell us about Jesus's nature when He was born? Why is this important?**

# display |

Mary knew that obeying God could destroy her reputation among those who did not believe the miracle. From the moment the angel showed up, she was troubled (v. 29), but she trusted and obeyed God anyway. When you encounter social rejection because you hold to a Christian worldview, remember this text. When your heart is pounding because the class discussion has opened a door to confess Christ, remember these verses. If it comes to it, sacrifice your reputation or good standing for the sake of the gospel. Obey God anyway. With Him, nothing is impossible (v. 37).

Holy Spirit of God, I see Your ministry on display in these verses. You did the Father's will, and the sinless Savior came into the world as a result. Lead the days of my life, God of the impossible. May what You have spoken over me come to pass (see v. 38).

**DAY 22**

# THE PUZZLE CLICK

## discover |

READ LUKE 4:1-15.

*Then Jesus returned to Galilee in the power of the Spirit, and*
*news about him spread throughout the entire vicinity.*
*—Luke 4:14*

Let's be honest, there aren't many more satisfying feelings than clicking
a puzzle piece into place. As the puzzle comes together, it's exciting
to see the picture take shape. Sometimes a piece gets placed, but as
everything starts to take shape around it, it turns out it's actually not
supposed to go there. This is what happens when Scripture is used out
of context. It might seem like it works, but ultimately it doesn't.

Verse 1 frames the whole event. Satan had a strategy. He had three
specific attacks he would use on Jesus. He even used Scripture, trying
to be tricky. But you can't trick the Author of life. Now, observe as the
Trinity goes to work.

This famous passage of Jesus overcoming temptation on a scale
beyond what we will ever know began with the Holy Spirit and it ended
with Jesus victorious over the devil. Satan used Scripture out of context
to tempt Jesus, and Jesus responded with Scripture properly in context.
He was filled with the Holy Spirit, who inspired the words of Scripture.
Satan tried to push the puzzle pieces in ways they were not intended.
Jesus used the Word as intended. The result is the satisfying click of
a piece of the puzzle fitting correctly into place, and a moment of
temptation was conquered.

*Three-In-One*

# delight |

The Spirit led Jesus into the situation where He would be tempted. Why would this be necessary for Jesus?

Let's be clear: God does not tempt us (see James 1:13). So why is it necessary that we face temptation? How do we overcome temptation?

# display |

Respond to temptation the way Jesus did—with Scripture in accordance with its original context, filled with the Holy Spirit as you do. When Satan tempts you, proclaim the sacred words of the Bible as God intended them. Invite the same Holy Spirit who fueled Jesus's ministry to set you free.

**Holy Spirit of God who filled the Son to the glory of the Father, fill my heart and life. Deliver me from evil. Give me words from Scripture when temptation comes, used according to their context as Jesus rightly used them. Cover my life, Holy Spirit.**

# THE OVERFLOW

## discover |

READ JOHN 7:37-39.

*He said this about the Spirit. Those who believed in Jesus were going to receive the*
*Spirit, for the Spirit had not yet been given because Jesus had not yet been glorified.*
*—John 7:39*

Have you ever seen a preview for a movie that you knew was coming out
and were very excited about, only to get to the end and read the words,
"Coming soon"? When is soon? That could be next month or next year! The
wait for something awesome can be painfully tantalizing, and you wish you
could skip forward in time to enjoy it. What Jesus taught about the Holy
Spirit in today's verses, however, is happening right this very second—no
waiting necessary. It is also infinitely better than your favorite movie; it is the
living water of the Holy Spirit. He is here!

The Holy Spirit first poured out on the church in Acts 2. What Jesus foretold
in today's verses has come to pass. What He prophesied has come to pass in
every believer for the last two thousand years. We have all had access to this
fountain of Living Water.

As He spoke these words, however, Jesus still had work to do before the
Spirit would come reside in believers as He does today. This incredible gift
of the Holy Spirit came at an incredible cost. Jesus's death, resurrection, and
ascension had to come first. Since this has happened, we now enjoy the
overflow of the Holy Spirit in our lives.

# delight |

Jesus described Himself as living water and now the Holy Spirit as living water. How can both the Son and the Spirit be Living Water?

According to verse 38, does belief in Jesus as merely a moral teacher, or even just as a worker of miracles, bring the Living Water of the Holy Spirit? Explain.

# display |

Invite someone new to the Living Water. Our bodies need and crave physical water, but our souls need and crave this Living Water even more. This Living Water is not found in anything or anyone else; life is not found in worldly views or habits. Invite them to the fountain. Pray that the Holy Spirit draws on their hearts. Ask them what they believe, listen intently, then share your story. Let the living water flow and seize the moment if the Holy Spirit opens the opportunity to pray Romans 6:23 and Romans 10:9 with them.

Holy Spirit, flow in my soul like Living Water. Overflow to reach the people in my life who are far from God to bring them all home. Go before me in time to prepare a moment of conviction and miraculous repentance. Bring my friends home, Jesus.

## DAY 24

# THE COUNSELOR IS IN

## discover |

READ JOHN 14:15-17.

*"And I will ask the Father, and he will give you*
*another Counselor to be with you forever."*
*—John 14:16*

People are more open about mental health than at any time in history. This is a good thing, and counseling is vitally important. Since this is true, why, in spite of the rise in society's willingness to talk about mental health, do things not seem to be getting better? Because the only thing that truly transforms a person is the Holy Spirit. Yes, counseling and therapy help, but the greatest Counselor of all is the Spirit of God living inside us.

He is with us forever (see v. 16) and His office is open twenty-four hours a day. The world around us does not understand His counsel (see v. 17), but those who confess Jesus as Lord know Him well. Jesus's first words in this passage are important because many of the things for which we seek counsel were brought on by our own disobedience. Because we know Jesus, we have the Holy Spirit within our very beings (v. 17). As wonderful as human counselors can be, none of them are the Spirit of truth Himself like the Holy Spirit is (v. 17).

Let's be perfectly clear; the Holy Spirit can use and speak to you through counselors. But it's important that we choose the right type of counselors so we do not receive mixed messages.

# delight |

**How does the counsel we receive from the world differ from the counsel of the Holy Spirit?**

**Based on verse 16, describe each Person of the Trinity's role in the outpouring and indwelling of the Holy Spirit within believers.**

# display |

Journal to the Holy Spirit the things in your life for which you need His counsel. Lay them out in brutal honesty. Pour out your heart to the Counselor and ask for His peace to overwhelm your anxious heart. Pray with a new fervency you have never before expressed. Experience the peace He brings. What Jesus foretold about the Spirit is present today. The rate He charges per hour is $0; He does not require insurance; He keeps all things perfectly confidential; and the wisdom He gives has been perfect for eternity.

Wonderful Counselor, Almighty God, bring Your perfect peace to my aching heart. You are the Spirit of truth and I believe You. I do not want counsel that tells me to keep on sinning. Thank you, Jesus, for asking the Father to bring the Counselor to my heart.

*Three-In-One*

## MEMORY VERSE

John 16:13

"When the Spirit of truth comes, he will guide you into all the truth. For he will not speak on his own, but he will speak whatever he hears. He will also declare to you what is to come."

# YOU KNOW IT TO BE TRUE

## discover |

READ JOHN 15:26-27.

*"When the Counselor comes, the one I will send to you from the Father —the Spirit of truth who proceeds from the Father—he will testify about me. "*
*—John 15:26*

When *The Empire Strikes Back* came out in 1980 (I know, ancient history) and it was revealed that Darth Vader was Luke Skywalker's father, if there had been an internet then, it would have been broken. But there was a problem. People didn't believe it! They thought it was a lie Vader was using to trick Luke. So George Lucas, creator of Star Wars, had to write a scene in the next movie, *The Return of the Jedi*, to convince people it was true. Obi-Wan Kenobi and Yoda, two of the most trustworthy characters in the story, confirmed the truth about Vader and Luke. It took trustworthy sources to convince the audience of what was true.

In today's verses, Jesus said the Spirit, who comes from the Father, will testify about Him. What this means is that all Jesus said about Himself would be verified by the Spirit. There is no disunity within the Trinity. There is only love and truth. Therefore, we can believe with all our hearts what the Spirit tells us about Jesus.

Notice the three Persons of the Trinity at work in these two short verses. Jesus sent the Spirit. The Spirit proceeds from the Father. You join in the work of the Spirit. There can be no higher or more trustworthy calling in our lives than this.

# delight

What are the ways the Holy Spirit speaks to us? How do we know what the Spirit is saying to us is true?

These verses immediately follow a warning from Jesus to His disciples that some people would hate them (see vv. 18-25). The same is true for us today. How do we continue to stand for what is true even if the world hates us?

# display |

We can trust God because He has proven Himself trustworthy and true time and time again. This is something we should mimic. Look inside yourself. Are you a trustworthy person? Do you do what you say you will do? Do you honor your promises? Do you keep your word? When you are given a task, do you seek to accomplish it with excellence? If you have a hard time saying yes to any of these questions, don't let it discourage you—we are all works in progress. However, don't stay the same. Seek to become a trustworthy person. List three things you can do right now to help you become a more trustworthy person.

Counselor, You have been testifying the truth of who Jesus is from the beginning. I will join with You in this testifying ministry. I am not ashamed. I am not afraid. I am not alone. Holy Spirit, let me know that I am with You.

# NO ONE LIKES SHOTS

## discover |

READ JOHN 16:1-11.

*"Nevertheless, I am telling you the truth. It is for your benefit that I go away, because if I don't go away the Counselor will not come to you. If I go, I will send him to you."*
*—John 16:7*

Jesus's words to His disciples before the crucifixion were life and truth, but they were hardly comforting. The disciples were heartbroken to hear that Jesus would be leaving them, but Jesus knew it was better for them that He die on the cross, rise again, and ascend to heaven (see v. 7).

It's sort of like when you're sick and have to go to the doctor. Sometimes you need a shot of Penicillin or an antibiotic to get better. It might be scary and painful to receive the shot, but ultimately, it will help you get well. No one likes to get a shot, but it's necessary, and that's the disciples' situation in these verses.

Though Jesus was departing from His disciples, He was not leaving them. He was sending them the Holy Spirit. Today, if you follow Jesus, He is with you. Jesus completed His earthly ministry and ascended. Today, the Holy Spirit lives in every believer. Though we as Christians are imperfect, the Holy Spirit within us is perfect just as Jesus is perfect.

# delight

After reading verses 1-4, what should be the expectation for how living a Christian life should go?

According to Jesus's words in verses 8 and 9, what three things does the Holy Spirit convict the world about and why does He do it?

# display |

Re-read verse 2 again. Sometimes we as Christians are terrible to one another—especially online. The people who persecuted the early followers of Jesus thought they were doing God's work, but that was because they didn't know Him (see v. 3). What do we need to do when we face criticism from within the family of faith? Bring two gigantic buckets of grace with you. We as Christians should be the most grace-filled people in the world. So, make sure that their criticism isn't true. If it is, repent. But if you are facing ugliness or mean-spiritedness from within your faith family, use the first bucket of grace on them. Accept what is true, reject what is false, forgive, and walk with the Spirit. The second bucket of grace is for you. There will be times when you'll need it as well.

Holy Spirit, I thank You for convicting me of my sin. I thank You for convicting me to be more righteous. I thank You for bringing ultimate justice in eternity while evil still affects this world (see vv. 9-11). Help me to remember Jesus's warning and show grace, especially to my church.

# OLD POSTS

## discover |

READ JOHN 16:12-15.

*"When the Spirit of truth comes, he will guide you into all the truth. For he will not speak on his own, but he will speak whatever he hears. He will also declare to you what is to come."*
—*John 16:13*

Every few months it seems there is an actor, comedian, or celebrity in trouble because someone finds a social media post from years ago that isn't considered to be funny or politically correct today. They have to delete the post, go on a weeks-long or sometimes months-long apology tour, then hope they don't get canceled forever so they can continue to have a career.

There is a reason why some old social media posts do not age well. Our culture's sense of truth is based on relativism—the idea that truth changes over time. What culture says is true isn't necessarily true. What is considered to be virtuous this week might be morally repugnant the next. You just never know. In today's verses, Jesus explained that the Holy Spirit guides us into truth that doesn't change like the tide.

Consider this: among the eleven disciples who heard Jesus say the words from today's verses, John wrote not only this gospel, but also the books of 1, 2, and 3 John along with Revelation. Peter wrote the books of 1 and 2 Peter. This tells us that the words Jesus said to them remained true and weren't later revealed as false. This is because the Holy Spirit illuminates our hearts as we read the words of Scripture and confirms their truth for all time.

## delight |

In verse 12 Jesus said He had more to share with the disciples, but they weren't ready to hear it. Why is it best that God doesn't tell us everything upfront?

Where do you see the unity of the Trinity in John 16:12-15?

# display |

As we've already stated, what is true gets muddy in our world today. However, the truth the Spirit shares from God's Word remains. Memorize John 16:13 so you can be reminded of what is really true as you navigate the choppy waters of this present world.

God, You spoke through Your Son. You speak through Your Holy Spirit. The very truth embodied by Jesus (see John 14:6) has been put into writing by the inspiration of the Spirit. Spirit, show opportunities and give me Scripture to share with someone in need today.

# GO AHEAD AND KNOCK

## discover |

READ LUKE 11:5-13.

*"If you then, who are evil, know how to give good gifts to your children, how much more will the heavenly Father give the Holy Spirit to those who ask him?"*
*—Luke 11:13*

Hospitality was crucially important in Jesus's day. Put yourself in the situation He described in these verses. You have people coming over to your house and you have nothing to offer them. What would you do? Go next door and say, "Open up, man! I've got people coming over and I have no food. Help me out!" Even though our culture is different, I think we can relate to the point Jesus was trying to get across.

In Jesus's first parable (see vv. 5-10), we are called to show shameless boldness in knocking on God's door in prayer to ask for the things we need. In Jesus's second parable (see vv. 11-13), we get to see God's perspective on our prayers. If you were a parent and your child asked for cereal, you would not give her rusty nails. You would never do that! If we know how to give good gifts in spite of our sin nature, just imagine God's heart toward His children asking Him for the Holy Spirit. So what are you waiting for? Go ahead and knock.

# delight |

What drove the neighbor in Jesus's first parable out of bed to help his noisy friend? What does that teach us about prayer?

Even though all people are born with a sin nature, we still have traces of our original design from God imprinted on our hearts. When have you seen someone who does not know God do the right thing?

# display |

Ask. Seek. Knock. As you follow Jesus's instructions on praying, watch as your prayer life takes off. Ask God to have His will done in your life. Seek deliverance from temptation. Knock and pound shamelessly on His door, asking the Father to pour out the Holy Spirit. Knock and ask Him to give you what you need. Knock and ask forgiveness for every last one of your sins and it will be given. He desires for you to talk to Him and to listen to Him.

Father, Your name is honored because You are holy, above everything else. Bring Your heavenly kingdom into my earthly situation. Give me what I need today. I desire to forgive everyone who has sinned against me. Please, forgive my sins and direct my life away from temptation.

# EMPOWERED

## discover |

READ LUKE 24:44-53.

*"And look, I am sending you what my Father promised. As for you, stay in the city until you are empowered from on high."*
*—Luke 24:49*

They thought He was a ghost. The resurrected Jesus crashed a party including the eleven remaining disciples and two other believers (called "disciples" in vv. 13-35) who had just come seven miles from Emmaus that evening to tell them they had seen the risen Jesus. Jesus showed them His wounds from the cross and even ate some fish to prove He was not a ghost but resurrected and real (see Luke 24:37-43).

Having established His non-ghost status, Jesus had something to say. Anything stated by a miraculously resurrected, fish-eating non-ghost is important. They had heard Him prophesy His death and resurrection before, but this time He himself opened their minds to really grasp it (see v. 45). Verse 49 then included their marching orders. They were to wait in the city—which was no small task since they were not in friendly territory and were currently being framed by the Jewish religious authorities for faking the resurrection (see Matt. 28:11-15). The empowerment from on high Jesus told them they would receive from the Father in verse 49 was and is the Holy Spirit you have today.

# delight

**What three Old Testament sources did Jesus say foretold His suffering and resurrection?**

**Before ascending to heaven (see vv. 50-53) at the very close of Luke's Gospel, Jesus promised to send the Holy Spirit. Why is it important that He sent the Holy Spirit?**

# display |

As foretold in the Law of Moses (Genesis-Deuteronomy), the Prophets (Ezekiel-Malachi) and the Psalms; the repentance for forgiveness of sins made possible by Jesus's prophesied suffering and resurrection is to be proclaimed to all the nations (see v. 47). Ask your ministry leader about your church's involvement in global missions. Ask for specific ways to pray for global missions ministries and talk to your parent or guardian about what you can give to global missions. In tomorrow's devotion, we will look at the global scale of Jesus's ministry again. Today, we pray and give to proclaim Jesus in every nation (see v. 47).

Jesus, You sent Your disciples' power from on high and dispatched them to the nations. Today, Holy Spirit, You dwell in every believer as we bring the gospel to the world. Without Your empowerment, His mission is impossible. Fill me, Holy Spirit, and empower our missionaries.

# THE ULTIMATE COMMISSION

## discover |

READ MATTHEW 28:16-20.

*Jesus came near and said to them, "All authority has been given to me in heaven and on earth. Go, therefore, and make disciples of all nations, baptizing them in the name of the Father and of the Son and of the Holy Spirit, teaching them to observe everything I have commanded you. And remember, I am with you always, to the end of the age."*
—Matthew 28:18-20

Have you ever noticed that just before you go on a trip somewhere without your parents or guardians, they try to tell you "just one more thing"? This is Jesus's "just one more thing." And it's a big one. This is called The Great Commission. It is the marching orders for all Christ-followers, for all time, at all places. It's a big deal! And notice who all shows up here—each Person of the Trinity.

It is in obedience to verse 18 that some Christian missions organizations will break nation's laws prohibiting the spread of the gospel. Jesus gave this passage, with all the combined authority of heaven and earth, so by God's standard, it supercedes the laws of nations that forbid it.

Jesus told His followers to practice baptism. This helps set us apart from everyone else because we are baptized in the name of the Father, Son, and Holy Spirit. The aim of Jesus's followers is to teach everyone, everywhere all that God commanded. Our hearts are emboldened by Jesus's final promise in verse 20. No matter how crazy the world gets, He is with us always (see v. 20).

# delight |

In verse 19, Jesus told disciples to become disciple-makers. How do you grow as a disciple of Jesus?

How can you help others grow as disciples of Jesus?

Why would some of the eleven disciples see the miracles of Jesus and the crucifixion of Jesus, then meet the resurrected Jesus on a mountain in Galilee; but still doubt (see v. 17)?

# display

Follow through with baptism if you have not already. Your baptism proclaims the burial and resurrection of Christ (see Rom. 6) and proclaims each Person of the Trinity! Having prayed for global missions and given to global missions, talk with your ministry leader about opportunities for you to go on a global missions trip. This Commission began on a different hemisphere and continent than the one you are (most likely) on right now. Now here you are on the other side of the world, a follower of Jesus because generations of people were faithful to this commission. Will you be faithful to do with those who came before you do and go into all the world and share the good news?

Even to the end of the age, You are with me, Jesus. You gave this commissioning with the ultimate authority. Who am I to disregard it? Father, by your Holy Spirit, draw my friends to your Son. Use me to make Your name great in the nations!

# Invited

When Jesus invited the disciples, saying, "Follow me," He wasn't just talking about following Him down a dusty road between Galilee and Jerusalem. He was talking about every aspect of their lives. The invitation wasn't "Walk where I walk"; it was Jesus saying, "Do what I do." And this holy invitation is extended to you too.

While it might feel like we're at a disadvantage because we can't follow Jesus physically like the first disciples, we have the Spirit of God dwelling within us and God's written Word to guide us in following Jesus and growing our relationship with God. He invites us into the unity He shares with the Father and Spirit.

Before you begin reading and responding to the Scripture below, ask the Holy Spirit to guide you in your time of study. Then, come and see how Jesus invites us to follow Him as we . . .

## Glorify God

READ JOHN 14:1-4.

Jesus didn't ask for glory for Himself for selfish reasons; in everything He did, Jesus gave glory to the Father, acknowledging God as the One who sent Him and gave Him authority over all people—including us. Here, Jesus specifically pointed out that He glorified God by completing the work God had given Him to do. But Jesus's entire life was lived to the glory of God. Ours should be too.

READ JOHN 15:8; 1 CORINTHIANS 6:20; 10:31; AND EPHESIANS 2:10.

**Highlight in your Bible ways these verses show you what it means to glorify and honor God. Describe how you can apply one of these truths to your life.**

## Submit to God

READ JOHN 5:30 AND LUKE 22:42.

Jesus turned water into wine, calmed a raging sea, healed the sick, and raised the dead—and all of it was God's will. So was Jesus dying on the cross for our sins. Even in the most excruciating of moments, Jesus confirmed aloud that He would submit to God above His own desires.

READ JAMES 4:7; ROMANS 12:1-2; AND 1 PETER 5:6.

**Each of these verses reveals something about submitting to God. How can you live out what you learn from these verses?**

## Give Thanks to God

READ MATTHEW 14:19; 15:36; LUKE 10:21-24; 22:14-20; JOHN 11:38-44.

Jesus thanked God many times throughout His ministry—when He multiplied food to feed a lot of people, when God opened the hearts and minds of His disciples to see the truth, when God heard His prayer for Lazarus, and at the first Lord's Supper as He spent time with friends just before His crucifixion. For every good thing, Jesus gave thanks to the One who gave it.

READ 1 THESSALONIANS 5:18 AND JAMES 1:17.

**What does Jesus's example teach us about giving thanks? How do these verses help us understand that more?**

# Trust God

READ JOHN 5:20; 15:9; AND 1 PETER 2:21-24.

Jesus trusted in God's love, His promises, and His justice. Jesus trusted God, period. To the point that when He knew the Father's will was for Him to go to the cross—and there was no other way—He went willingly. Jesus's absolute trust in God shows us we can trust Him in every way too.

READ PHILIPPIANS 4:19; JOHN 14:1; ROMANS 8:28.

**How does Jesus's trust in God inspire you to trust Him more? What role does the rest of Scripture and your personal experience play in trusting God?**

# Treasure God's Word

READ MATTHEW 4:1-11; 22:37-40; 22:29; LUKE 2:41-52; 4:21; 16:16-17; AND JOHN 5:39-40; 10:35.

From the time He was a child, Jesus knew the importance of hearing Scripture. He quoted it when Satan tempted Him in the desert, and when religious leaders tried to trap Him in a lie, He pointed to it as the foundation of knowledge, acknowledged its authority and inerrancy, and used it to reveal God to a hurting world. Jesus showed people what it meant to treasure God's Word, to honor it as holy and valuable. And in that, He teaches us to do the same.

READ MATTHEW 4:4; JOHN 14:15; 17:17; AND 2 TIMOTHY 3:16-17.

**Why is it important to treasure God's Word? When do you struggle to do so?**

# Find Our Purpose in God

READ MATTHEW 3:17; 9:35; LUKE 4:17-20; AND JOHN 3:16-18; 4:34.

Jesus knew who He was—God's beloved Son—and His purpose. He came to do God's will, which was to teach, to heal, to set free, and ultimately, to save. He never wavered, even with persecution, threats of death, and eventually, dying on the cross. We who trust in Him are set free from sin for His good works. While we can't save others or set them free, we can share the gospel—the truth that trusting in Jesus does all of those things.

READ MATTHEW 6:33; JOHN 1:12; 20:21; ACTS 1:8; 2 CORINTHIANS 5:17; EPHESIANS 2:10; 1 PETER 2:9.

**How is Jesus's purpose different from ours? How is it similar? Why is it important for us to know who we are as we live out God's plan for our lives?**

# NOTES